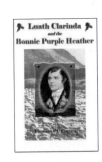

DVD available at: **www.insideasnowdrop.com**

Introduction

On the 22nd of June 1987, Scots poet and author, Tam Craven's life changed forever. Whilst working as a bricklayer on the Lennox Kincaid Mausoleum in Campsie Glen, he suffered a near fatal accident. Tam fell twenty two feet from a scaffold, fracturing his skull and right knee, breaking his ribs and puncturing a lung - apart from that and in his own words"...he was alright!..." Within a few years his life began to take another direction and today he is working on his 22nd collection of poems and short stories. Deeply inspired by the writings of Robert Burns, Tam's work takes a contemporary look at life in Scotland - often as it happens and always straight from the heart! Most of all Tam enjoys making people laugh! Not content with writing and publishing, Tam relishes taking his work direct to the public, whether at fairs, spoken word events or bookshops. Tam has been interviewed and recited a selection of his work live on radio in Scotland, Spain and in Victoria BC. Tam is the poet in residence at the world famous Loch Lomond Shores and recent live appearances in Scotland have included the 'Aye write' festival in Glasgow and the 'Whiskey an' a' that' festival in Ayr. Through his work and performances, Tam regularly supports charitable organisations in Scotland. Duncan Gilchrist lives in Milton of Campsie and works in the newspaper industry.

THE COLLABORATORS

TAM CRAVEN   DUNCAN GILCHRIST

MY WINDAES ARE STEAMIN' 'N' SO AM A

A SWALLEED A DICTIONARY
JUST THE OTHER DAY
AND DIGESTED IT SLOWLY
AND IT CAME OUT OKAY

THEN A DRANK A BOTTLE O' WHISKY
AND ARGUED WI' M'SEL
AND REMEMBERED INEBRIATION
NAE WONDER AM NO' WELL

WELCOME TO THE LAND OF AILMENTS
AND THE ALE MANS COUNTRY
IF IT WUSNY FOR A WEE DRAP O' BEER
WHERE THE HELL WOULD WE BE

AND NOO MY WINDAES ARE STEAMIN'
AND SO AM A
THE STEAK PIES BEEN BURNED
A'LL NEED TAE CLOSE THE BAR

AND NOO M' WIFE'S RAN AWA'
WI' ANITHER MAN'S WIFE
AND AH'LL BE PEELING TOTTIES
FOR THE REST O' M' LIFE

I wrote this wan when I was full o'the drink, thank God I'm an atheist April the 5th 2007.

BIG FAYE FAE FAIFLEY

I AM OFFAY AU FAIT
WI' BIG FAYE FAE FAIFLEY
WE'RE GON FOR A PINT THE NIGHT
THEN WE'LL POP IN TAE SAFEWAY

THEN ME 'N' BIG FAYE
WE'LL HUV A ROLL IN THE HAY
AN' EFTER A WEE WHILE
SHE'LL SEND ME AWAY

THEN SHE'LL PHONE ME UP
THE VERY NEXT DAY
AND TELL ME SHE LOVES ME
THAT'S M' BIG FAYE

THAT'S WHY AM OFFAY AU FAIT
WI' BIG FAYE FAE FAIFLEY
COS SHE ALWAYS PHONES ME UP
THE VERY NEXT DAY

Written on the 18th April 2007, ye canny whack the daft wans eh!

AFFLUENZA

A WENT TAE SEE M' DOCTOR
JOOST THE OTHER DAY
HE LOOKED ME UP AND DOWN AND SAID
BIG MAN, YIR IN AN OFFAY BAD WAY

YIV CAUGHT A BAD DISEASE
IT'S CALLED AFFLUENZA
YOU BETTER CHANGE YOUR WAYS
AFORE IT GOES TOO FAR

YIR WORKING EIGHTEEN HOURS A DAY
FOR THE SAKE O' GREED GREED GREED
YOU BETTER STOAP CHASIN' MONEY
COS YIR GONNY END UP DEID

HOW MANY SUITS DO YOU NEED
HOW MANY CARS CAN YOU DRIVE
WE ONLY NEED ONE SHROUD YOU KNOW
WE'RE ONLY HERE TO SURVIVE

SO GET YOUR LIFE THE GITHER M' FRIEND
STOAP CHASIN' AVARICE AND WEALTH
AND GET RID OF THIS AFFLUENZA
AND START THINKIN' OF YIR HEALTH

How many people do you know who are in love with money, plenty eh! I once knew a guy down in Manchester who was obsessed with making money, that's all he could talk about, night and day, day and night and probably in his sleep....   THEN HE DIED

4

THE CONSTANT KNOWING

"GET YIR FAGS 'N' TABAKKA HERE"
HE RELEASED FAE THE CORNER O' HIS GUB
"KEEP YIR EYE OOT FUR THE POLIS SON
AM JOOST NICKIN' IN TAE THE PUB"

AND THE POLIS WALK ROON IN CIRCLES
MAKIN' OOT THAT THEY REALLY CARE
AND THE DEALERS COONT THEIR MONEY
FOR THEY AINT GOIN' ANYWHERE

AND THE JUDGES AND THE LAWYERS
KEEP OAN RAKIN' THE MONEY IN
AND THE FOLK WHO WANT A BARGAIN
ARE TOLD THEY'RE COMMITTING A SIN

DRAG ON DRAG ON THROUGH THIS LIFE
AND TELL ME WHY DO PEOPLE WANT TAE SMOKE
MAYBE IT IS THE CONSTANT KNOWING
THAT THIS LIFE IS BUT A JOKE

AND THE POLIS KEEP WALKING ROON IN CIRCLES
MAKIN' OOT THAT THEY REALLY CARE
AND PEOPLE ARE GONNY DIE ANYWAY
AND GOD IS EVERYWHERE

Written on May 7th 2007. The day before I was in the Barras in Glasgow and there was a load of polis here there and everywhere trying to "stop illegal activity". What a joke, why don't they admit that they cannot stop smuggling, it is almost impossible, it has been going on for hundreds of years. Or maybe they do not want to stop it, now there's a thought.

SERENITY

YOU CANNY BUY THIS SERENITY
LYING BACK OAN THE CAMPSIE FELLS
WHILST SAYING A PRAYER FOR HUMANITY
AND LISTENING TO ST MACHAN'S BELLS

FAR FROM ARGUMENTS AND HASSLE
YET ONLY A MILE AWAY
I LOOK DOWN WITH DELIGHTED PLEASURE
AND THANK GOD I GO MY OWN WAY

I SEE FALL OUTS AND FIGHTS EVERY OTHER DAY
AND PEOPLE LASHING OUT WITH THEIR IRE
WHAT A DELIGHT IT IS TO HAVE PEACE AND SERENITY
AND TO MY CAMPSIES I DO ASPIRE

WHY IS EVERYBODY IN A HURRY
AND EVERYONE THINKS THEY ARE RIGHT
THEY CAN ARGUE AND RUSH A' THEY WANT MY FRIEND
FOR THE MEIKLE BIN TO ME, IS A FAR BETTER SIGHT

I CAUGHT THAT FISH !

SOMETIMES I FEEL QUITE UNEASY ABOUT
THAT IMAGINED SELF OF MINE
ONE WHERE I LEAD A THEATRICAL LIFE
AND WALK A DIFFERENT LINE

ONE DAY I SHADOWED HIM DOWN THE STREET
WHERE HE STOOD AT A SHOP WINDOW
AND DRESSED HIMSELF IN GREEN
VELVET AND FLORAL TIE
THEN BOUGHT A ROLLS ROYCE AND A GRAND PIANO

HELD GRAND PARTIES EVERY OTHER NIGHT
WITH WINE WOMEN AND SONG
HAD LAZY DAYS AT THE RACES
BACKING WINNERS ALL DAY LONG

THEN SUDDENLY HE SOLD ALL HIS BELONGINGS
FOR BEING RICH AND FAMOUS HAD LOST IT'S ALLURE
THEN HE SAVED A DOG FROM BEING DROWNED
THEN LED A LIFE OF SELF SACRIFICE AMONG THE POOR

I BEGAN TO FEEL QUITE ENCOURAGED ABOUT HIM
FOR ALTHOUGH I COULD ONLY WISH
FOR WHEN PASSING A FISHMONGER'S WINDOW,
HE POINTED AT A GREAT SALMON AND SHOUTED,
"I CAUGHT THAT FISH!"

Written on the 24th of June 2007. Is not the brain and imagination the most wonderful thing that God has created.

TWO DAFFODILS

TWO DAFFODILS HAD FALLEN IN LOVE
HANGING OVER THE FOREVER BURN
THEIR PETALS CARESSING ONE AND OTHER
AS MY HEARTS MEMORY TOOK A TURN

THOSE MOMENTS ALL CAME FLOODING BACK
OF THE WALKS WE USED TO TAKE
AND AS I WATCH THE DAFFODILS KISS
I WISH THOSE TIMES COULD SOMEHOW AWAKE

ALL THE PROMISES AND VOWS MADE
LINGER FOREVER IN MY MIND
BUT IN YOUTH WE REALLY DON'T KNOW
OF THE THINGS WE SAID IN BLIND

AND SOON THE TWO DAFFODILS WILL GO
TO THEIR HONEYMOON UP IN THE SKY
AND THEY WILL COME BACK EVERY YEAR
WHILST US HUMANS CAN ONLY DIE

I wrote this one at Banks Farm after seeing two daffodils entangled with each other whilst dancing with the wind below the gorse and broom.

A PHEASANT PLUCKER

HE'S A POET, A PRINCE
AND A PHILOSOPHER
IN ALL HONESTY
HE'S A PHEASANT PLUCKER

HE SAID HE PLAYED GOLF IN JAMAICA
AND DANCED WI' FRED ASTAIRE
BUT TO ME HE'LL ALWAYS BE
A PHEASANT PLUCKER

HE SAID HE CLIMBED MOUNT EVEREST
AND WRESTLED WI' A BEAR
THATS NO' BAD GOIN'
FOR A PHEASANT PLUCKER

HE SAID HE MET THE QUEEN
AND HAD A RIGHT GOOD DRINK WI' HER
BUT A DON'T THINK LIZZIE WID DRINK
WI' A PHEASANT PLUCKER

HE SAID HE MET THE DALAI LAMA
AND HAD A RIGHT GID TERR
ME THINK'S HE'S CRACKIN UP
MY PHEASANT PLUCKER

HE SAYS HE BROKE THE WORLD RECORD
FOR EATING MINCE PIES
I THINK THE PHEASANT PLUCKER
DOTH TELL TO MANY LIES

BUT IN ALL HONESTY
HOW COULD I GO ELSEWHERE
FOR HE'S MY GREAT AULD PAL
HE'S MY PHEASANT PLUCKER

GOODBYE TO OLD CHESTER

WE GOT DONE BY ASCOT AT CHELTENHAM
AND DEVELOPED A HELLUVA THIRSK
SO ME AND MY FRIEND CHESTER
WE HEADED FOR LEICESTER
IN THE HOPE OF A FEW WINNERS

IN THE RED CAR WE WENT TO UTTOXETER
THEN TAUNTON AND MARKET RASEN
GOT DONE IN WINCANNOT
AND FELT LOW IN LUDLOW
NOW WHERE THE HELL DO WE GO

AFTER AN EARLY BATH
WE CAME UP FOR AYR
AND HAMILTON KELSO AND PERTH
WENT ON TO MUSSELBURY
IN A HELLUVA HURRY
BUT NEVER HAD ANY LUCK THERE

WE LUMPED ON AT PLUMPTON
AT CARLISLE AND CARTMEL
WHERE LADY LUCK WAS'NT SO WELL
WHAT THE FAKENHAM IS HAPPEN'
NAE WONDER CHESTER'S NOT WELL

STARTED A WAR IN WARWICK AND SOUTHWELL
AT WORCESTER AND WOLVERHAMPTON AS WELL
GOT RIPPED OFF AT RIPON BY A BOOKIE NAMED JOHN
AND GOT DINGED BY A BEVERLEY BELLE

GOT COLLARED AT SEDGFIELD AND SANDOWN
GOT STUFFED AT STRATFORD AS WELL
POOR CHESTER WAS PULLIN' HIS HAIR OOT
AND SALISBURY WAS PURE BLOODY HELL

WE BATTLED ON TO NEWMARKET
THEN NEWBURRY AND NEWTON ABBOT TOO
THE HORSES WERE SLOW
AND THOUGHT! HOW CAN THIS BE?
AND RAISED OUR GLASSES TO BANGOR-ON-DEE

IT SEEMS YE CANNY WIN AT WINDSOR,
OR YARMOUTH EXETER OR YORK,
NAE CHANCE O' WINNIN' AT LIVERPOOL,
THAT'S SURELY A MATTER O' PONTEFRACT.

AT HEREFORD HEXHAM AND HAYDOCK,
THE GOING WAS PRETTY TOUGH,
AND AFTER HUNTINGDON BRIGHTON AND
CHEPSTOW, WE'D SURELY HAD ENOUGH.

WE MANAGED A FEW WINNERS AT LINGFIELD,
AT FOLKSTONE WE HAD A GOOD TIME,
HAD A BIT OF A LARK AT OLD KEMPTON PARK,
WETHERBY ACCIDENT OR DESIGN.

BUT THEN! WE GOT TOASTED AT TOWCESTER,
AND THE SAME AT FONTWELL AS WELL,
WITH FURTHER BAD NEWS AT NEWCASTLE,
WHERE THREE "HONEST"' FAVOURITES FELL

THEN ALONG CAME CATTERICK AND FFOS LAS
AND NOTTINGHAM SO FAIR,
BUT WE SADLY MISSED EPSOM,
WE COULDN'T AFFORD TO GO THERE.

BUT MONEY WAS RAISED FOR GOODWOOD,
FROM **A**SCOT IN DONCASTER,
IF THE HORSES DON'T START TO WIN SOON,
THEN IT'S GOODBYE TO OLD CHESTER.

This poem includes the names of all 60 horse race tracks in mainland Great Britain

RUN LUATH RUN

RUN LUATH, RUN BOY
THROUGH YOUR BONNIE HILLS AND GLEN
RUN WHILE YOU'RE YOUNG BOY
THE CHANCE WON'T COME AGAIN

RUN MY SWIFT WEE COLLIE
THROUGH THE FIELDS AND O'ER THE BRAES
ENJOY YOUR SWIFT TIMES BOY
FOR YOUNG LIFE NEVER STAYS

RUN WITH YOUR SIX SENSES
ON TO YOUR FINAL HILL
THIS LIFE A CANNY MAKE SENSE O' IT
AND MAN, PROBABLY NEVER WILL

RUN LUATH, RUN BOY
THROUGH THE SEAS OF LIFES CORN
YOU DON'T HAE MONY CARES BOY
MAYBE THAT'S WHY MAN WAS BORN

RUN LUATH, RUN BOY
BE AS SWIFT AS YOU CAN BE
AND LEAVE US MORTAL HUMANS
WAITING ON LIBERTY

This one was written at 4.45am on 7th January 2005. Five hours earlier I had just finished reading "The Wind That Blows The Barley" by James Barke. The book is about the life and times of Robert Burns, the first in a series of five books. Near the end of the book the Bard is talking to his dog Luath about life and how quickly it all passes.

12

THE SEVEN WATERFALLS

MEET ME WHERE THE SEVEN WATERFALLS FLOW
AND WE'LL TALK OF DAYS GONE DOWN
AND DRINK FROM THE CUP OF MEMORIES
WHILST REMEMBERING FRIENDS WHO ARE NOT AROUND

THE LONG AGO DAYS OF YOUTH
THAT WE THOUGHT WOULD NEVER CEASE
NOW WE'RE BOTH OLD AND GREY
AND ALL WE SEEK IS PEACE

THOSE MAGICAL DAYS OF ADVENTURE
WITH NOT A CARE IN THE WORLD
BUT NOW LIFE'S FLAG IS AT HALF MAST
AND OUR DESTINY IS BEING UNFURLED

THROUGH LIFE'S MISTAKES AND FALL OUTS
WE STRUGGLED ON AND ON
WE'LL ALWAYS REGRET CERTAIN ONES
WE COULD HAVE ACTED BETTER UPON

SO LET US KEEP ON MEETING
WHERE THE SEVEN WATERFALLS FLOW
AND TREASURE THE DAYS WE HAVE LEFT
FOR THE FUTURE THAT WE DO NOT KNOW

Friday 8th of the 8th 2008, Antermony Loch 6.30pm.

THE RETURN OF NOAH'S ARK

ITS GONNY BE RAINING EVERYWHERE TODAY
EXCEPT FOR THE PLACES ITS GONNY BE DRY
BUT THE RAIN WILL BE WARM
SO THERE'S NO NEED TO CRY

THERE WILL BE HURRICANES IN HARROGATE
AND TORNADOS IN LONDON TOON
'N' FOLK WILL BE BLOWN UP IN TO THE SKY
'N' POWER LINES BLOWN DOON

THEN THE RAIN FROM SPAIN
WILL LASH DOON IN GLASGOW CITY
'N' BOATS WILL SAIL DOON SAUCHIEHALL STREET
OH WHAT A BLOODY PITY

AND THERE WILL BE GALES FROM THE NORTH
AND CYCLONES FROM THE WEST
'N' THE DUCKS WILL BE LAUGHING THEIR HEIDS AFF
FOR THE WEATHER THEY LOVE THE BEST

THEN NOAH'S ARK WILL EMERGE
FROM A DEEP WATTERY GRAVE
AND COME BACK FROM THE PAST
POOR MANKIND TO SAVE

CHAPPATIES OVER CAMPSIE

THE HAMILTON ACCIE
LIFTED A CHAPPATI
AND HUT ME O'ER THE HEID
AND SAID "GET UP BIG MAN
YOUR NO' DEID"

DO THAT AGAIN ALI
THAT WUS GREAT
TELL YIR DAUGHTER
NOT TO BE LATE

OCH! HIT ME WITH YIR CHAPPATI ALI
YIR A TRUE BLOODY SCOT
YOU MAKE ME LAUGH
YIR PATTERS RID HOT

COME ON UP TAE MA HOOSE
I'LL MAKE YOU HAGGIS 'N' NEEPS
FOLK WHO DON'T LIKE DARKIES
JUST GIVE ME THE CREEPS

KINDA FUNNY

AS I WALKED UP "ROON THE MOON"
I HEARD A CURLEW MOO
AND THOUGHT THAT KINDA FUNNY
THAT SURELY CANNY BE TRUE

TWAS THEN I SAW A RABBIT
FLYIN AFF A TREE
AND THOUGHT THAT KINDA FUNNY
THE CRAZY THINGS YOU SEE

AND THEN I SAW A SHEEP
PLAYING A GUITAR
AND THOUGHT THAT KINDA FUNNY
HE'D MABYE ONE DAY BE A STAR

FURTHER ON UP THE BRAES
A SEAGULL WAS DOIN' A TAP DANCE
HE WUSNY FRED ASTAIRE
BUT GEE THE BURD A CHANCE

THEN COMIN' DOON FROM "ROON THE MOON"
I REALISED THE CLINK (RHYME)
THERE WAS ONLY WAN ANSWER
LAY AFF THE DEMON DRINK

YOU'VE GOT TO LAUGH

IN THE END THE HANGOVERS WIN
AND YOU'VE GOT TO MAKE A DECISION
NOW IT'S SLOW HORSES AND SLOW WUMMIN
AND NIGHTS BY THE TELEVISION

An alcoholic is someone you don't like who drinks as much as you do.
Dylan Thomas 1965.

Work is the curse of the drinking classes.
Mike Romanoff.

17

THE POET THE LORRY ATE

THERE WAS A POET FROM AULD CAMPSIE TOUN
WHO RHYMED HIS LIFE AWAY
HE ALWAYS WROTE STRAIGHT FROM THE HEART
AND POMPOUS ARSEHOLES NEVER GOT IN HIS WAY

HE WAS IGNORED BY CERTAIN CRITICS OF THE DAY
AND THE ARTI FARTI FAE EDINBURRY
BUT HE WAS AN INDEPENDENT MAN
AND WAS CERTAINLY NOT IN ANY HURRY

HE WROTE THE 100 VERSE CLASSIC, "THROUGH AND THROUGH"
AND THE FUTURISTIC "LIGHTS OVER DONEGAL"
AND HE WALKED WITH HONESTY AND DIGNITY
EVEN AFTER A TERRIBLE FALL

THEN THERE WAS THE LOVELY POEM "THE WAY"
INSPIRED BY HIS MOTHER, ANNIE,
AND IF YOU TOLD HIM THERE'S SOMETHING THAT
HE COULD'NY DAE, WELL! HE'D JUST SAY "WHO CANNY!"

AND ALSO THERE'S THE FUNNY POEMS
"YOUNG LINDSAY YOUNG" AND "IT WUSNY ME"
WITH "THE LEEK" AND "BAKER BROON'S VAN"
THE MAN WUS OOOZIN WI' POETRY

BUT ONE DAY A BIG LORRY CAME ALANG
AND BY THEN IT WUS FAR TOO LATE
FOR HE'D BEEN SWALLOWED UP BY LIFE ITSEL'
THAT'S THE POET THE LAUREATE

The Poet Laureate is somebody who is allowed to write poetry for State
Occasions. Well! on several Occasions I have been in some States, I can
assure you my friends. So I have declared myself The Poet Laureate, of all
Scotland, at your service.
Cheers. Gies anither gless o' that wine.

THE AULD HOOSE COAL FIRE

I CANNOT THINK OF ANYTHING BETTER
ON A COLD WINTERS NIGHT
THAN SITTING BY THE AULD HOOSE COAL FIRE
DRINKING PINTS OF THE BLACK LIGHT

WITH FRIENDS AND FAMILY ALL AROUND
AND FACES BEAMING BY THE FIRELIGHT
TALKING AND LAUGHING AND SINGING SONGS
THOSE MEMORIES WERE SUCH A DELIGHT

AND I CHERISH EVERY ONE OF THOSE DAYS
WHEN EVERYTHING SEEMED TO BE JUST RIGHT
AND I STILL FEEL THE HEAT OF THE FIRE
AS I DREAM OF THE LOVELY BLACK LIGHT

BUT NOW THE MEMORY IS A DYING EMBER
OF THE AULD HOOSE COAL FIRE
AND HOW LUCKY I WAS TO HAVE BEEN THERE
IT WAS A TREASURE THAT FILLED MY DESIRE

The Auld Hoose pub, Lennoxtown.

THE LOST POET

A POET HAS BEEN LOST
ON HIS WAY TO SMOOTH RADIO
HE WAS SUPPOSED TO BE ON LIVE
ON THE DAVE MARSHALL SHOW

HE TOOK THE WRANG TURN
AFF THE M8 MOTORWAY
OH WHERE OH WHERE CAN HE BE
THIS POET OF THE DAY

WILL YE NO' COME BACK AGAIN
OOR TAM, TAE SMOOTH RADIO
AND GI'E THE FOLK A WEE LAUGH
ON THE DAVE MARSHALL SHOW

WD 40 M.O.T.EESE'S

THERE'S NO MORE NEED FOR DOCTORS
THERE'S NO MORE NEED FOR PILLS
FOR THE WONDROUS WD 40
HAS PANACEAD ALL KNOWN ILLS

MEN WHO ARE IN THEIR NINETIES
ARE NOW AS FIT AS FLEAS
AND WOMEN IN THEIR EIGHTIES
ARE SWINGIN' FAE THE TREES

THERE'S NAE MERR NEED FOR HOSPITALS
AN' NAE MERR DIRTY ROTTEN DISEASE'S
NOW FOLK JUST GO TAE THEIR LOCAL GARAGES
TAE GET THEIR PHYSICAL M.O.T.EESEE'S

THE HUMAN RACE WILL NEVER BE THE SAME
FOR THERE'S NO MORE COFFEE OR TEA
SO MAKE YIR WAY TO THE BAR MY FRIENDS
THE WD 40'S ARE ON ME

I went to visit Tommy Lamont an old friend of mine who will be ninety one on his next birthday.He told me he had arthritis in his shoulders and he was using WD40 to ease the pain, well I was dumbstruck. I thought he was pullin' ma leg. But he wusny, apparently it works and there are quite a few people using it. People are using it for all sorts of ailments, so I decided to spray some on to my hands and sat down at a piano and played the Warsaw Concerto from start to finish, nae bother, eat yir heart out Mr Addinsell!

A ROOM 'N' KITCHEN UP IN HEAVEN

AH'VE PUT M' NAME DOON
FUR A ROOM 'N' KITCHEN UP IN HEAVEN
AH'VE GOT A REALLY GOOD CHANCE O' GETTIN' IT
AS SOON AS A STOAP LIVIN'

THERE'S TOO MUCH OVERCROWDING HERE
WI' BUMPER TAE BUMPER MOTOR CARS
'N' A' THE FLOODIN' THAT'S GONNY COME
SOON MAN WILL HUV TAE FLY TAE THE STARS

HE HAS POLLUTED THIS LOVELY PLANET
WI' A' HIS LAZINESS AND GREED
AND NOW THERE'S NAE TURNIN' BACK
FOR THE GLACIERS ARE MELTING AT SPEED

AND IF THERE IS ANOTHER PLANET OUT THERE
THAT HUMAN BEINGS CAN GET TOO
YOU CAN BET YOUR BOTTOM DOLLAR
HE WILL DESTROY THAT ONE TOO

SO GET YIR NAME DOON RIGHT AWAY
FOR A ROOM 'N' KITCHEN IN NEVER NEVERLAND
'N' LET ME KNOW WHEN YIR FLITTIN'
'N' AH'LL COME 'N' GIE YE A HAND

Written at Banks Farm, Antermony Loch, 19th March 2008.

It takes in reality only one to make a quarrel. It is useless for the sheep to pass resolutions in favour of vegetarianism while the wolf remains of a different opinion.

W R Inge, Uotspoken essays 1919.

NEVER

HE THREW THE COMPUTER O'ER HIS SHOULDER
AND MARCHED THROUGH THE DOOR
THERE WUS NAEBODY LISTENING TO HIS WORDS
AND HE COULDNY TAKE IT NO MORE
DOON THE STREET HE THUNDERED
PAST OLD FRIENDS AND READERS GALORE
HE WID NEVER WRITE ANITHER WORD
HE WUS SICKENED TAE THE CORE
PAST THE SCHOOL WHERE HE WAS TAUGHT
WHERE THE PAGES OF LIFE TURN FAST
WHAT A WASTE OF TIME HE THOUGHT
A MIGHT AS WELL HUV BEEN LAST
HE'D BEEN THE DUX AND THE TEACHERS PET
AND A' THE LASSES HE COULD KISS
BUT NOO THE MEMORIES WERE SO BITTER
AS HE HEADED FOR THE ABYSS

HE STRODE PAST THE PUB
WHERE THE ETERNAL FURROW LED
HE WUS SICK TO HIS BACK TEETH WITH WORDS
NOW HIS COMPUTER WAS FOR A WATTERY BED
I COULD HAVE BEEN SOMEBODY
KEPT RINGING IN HIS EARS
AND AS HE NEARED THE GLAZERT RIVER
HE WAS FIGHTING BACK THE TEARS
JUST THEN HE SAW A YOUNG SALMON
TRYING TO CLIMB THE FALLS OF THE RIVER
AND SUDDENLY HIS HEART WAS FIRED UP
AS HE REMEMBERED THE WORD NEVER!
HE SAT THE COMPUTER ON THE BRIDGE
AND WATCHED THE YOUNG SALMON WIN
AND SAID TO HIMSELF HE'D NEVER GIVE IN
FOR THAT WOULD BE A TERRIBLE SIN
AND AS THE WATER FLOWS ON THE RIVER
HE WOULD LET THE WORDS FLOW FROM HIS HEART
AND EVEN IF NOBODY EVER READS THEM
THE TWO COULD NEVER BE APART

BAKER BROON'S VAN

"I FIND YOU GUILTY"
SAID THE JUDGE TO THE CAMPSIE MAN
"GUILTY OF STEALING THE STEAK PIES
FROM THE BACK OF BAKER BROON'S VAN"

"IT WUSNY ME THAT DONE IT
A DID'NY STEAL THE PIES
THE POLIS HUV SET ME UP
WI' TELLIN A LOAD O' LIES"

"BUT THE EVIDENCE IS SOLID
YOU WERE SEEN COMING OUT OF THE VAN
THEN YOU WENT TO THE BURNS TAVERN
WHERE YOU ORDERED A BLACK AND TAN"

"BUT A'HM TELLIN' YE YIR HONOUR
A'HM NOT GUILTY OF THIS CRIME
FOR A DON'T DRINK BLACK AND TANS
A DRINK LAGER AND LIME"

BUT THE JUDGE WAS DUE ON THE GOLF COURSE
AT A QUARTER PAST THREE
AND WAS FED UP LISTENING TO
THE THIEF FROM CAMPSIE

" I FINE YOU FIVE POUNDS
WITH ONE MONTH TO PAY
FOR I AM RUNNING LATE
THERE IS NOTHING MORE TO SAY"

SO AFTER GOLF BEER AND WHISKY
THE JUDGE TOLD HIS CRONIES ALL ABOUT THE CAMPSIE MAN
THEN THEY SAT DOWN TO EAT THE STEAK PIES
FROM THE BACK OF BAKER BROON'S VAN

This one was written on the 9th January at 6am, it just came to me. How it works I do not know.

'There's nae place like hame', quoth the De'il, when he found himself in the Court of Session.
Proverb
Hang a thief when he is young, and he'll no' steal when he is auld.
Lord Braxfield (1793 – 1799)

24

YOUNG LINDSAY YOUNG

WELL! YOUNG LINDSAY YOUNG
SHE STOLE THE FERMER'S DUNG
SHE EVEN HAD THE AUDACITY
TAE STEAL A COO'S TOUNGE

THEN FERMER BROON
WENT AFF HIS HEID
"WHEN A CATCH THESE CRIMINALS
A WILL CRACK THEIR HEIDS"

THEN YOUNG LINDSAY YOUNG
TRIED TAE SELL THE DUNG CHEAP
AND PROMISED EVERY BUYER
THAT THE DUNG WOULD KEEP

THEN THE POLIS THEY DID
GET WIND OF THE DUNG
BUT THEY NEVER SUSPECTED
YOUNG LINDSAY YOUNG

THEY SEARCHED NEAR AND FAR
OVER HILL AND DALE
BUT COULD NEVER FIND
THE DUNG FOR SALE

BUT FINALLY THE MASTER THIEF
WAS CAUGHT AND HELD FOR TRIAL
FOR YOUNG LINDSAY YOUNG
THERE WOULD BE NO DENIAL

SHE HIRED THE FAMOUS CHINESE
LAWYER CALLED, HOO FLUNG DUNG
WHO PROMISED THE EARLY RELEASE
OF YOUNG LINDSAY YOUNG

WELL! THE TRIAL DID START
AND IT WAS SUCH A FARCE
THE JUDGE WAS A FERMER
WI' A BIG FAT ARSE

AS THE TRIAL WENT ON
THERE WOULD BE NO DOUBT
THAT YOUNG LINDSAY YOUNG'S
TEA WOULD BE OUT

SHE WAS FINALLY FOUND
GUILTY AT LAST
AND EVERYBODY KNEW
OF HER LIFE IN THE PAST

AS SHE STOOD ON THE GALLOWS
WITH THE ROPE ROUND HER NECK
SHE SHOUTED UP TO HEAVEN
"HEY BIG MAN GIES A BREK"

THEN OUT OF THE BLUE
A WHITE HORSE DID ARRIVE
AND ON TO IT'S BACK
YOUNG LINDSAY DID DIVE

NOW THE MORAL OF THIS TALE
CAN NOW BE TOLD
DON'T EVER STEAL DUNG
EVEN THOUGH YOU ARE YOUNG OR OLD

AND SO LOOKING BACK
ON THIS TALE WITH HINDSIGHT
THE DUNG IS LIKE THIS POEM
JUST A LOAD OF SHIGHT

CAMPSIE MEN

TRYING TAE GET BLOOD OUT OF A RAVENOUS WOLVERINE
IS A VERY DIFFICULT THING TO DO, BUT!
IT WOULD BE EVEN HARDER TAE TAP A CAMPSIE MAN
WHO WUS STILL OAN THE BRU

MONEY IS HELLUVA TIGHT THESE DAYS
WI' THIS RECESSION AND THE CREDIT CRUNCH
'N' THERE'S NO' MUCH CHANCE O' A CAMPSIE MAN
TAKING YE OOT FOR YIR LUNCH

YEARS AGO A MET THREE SCOTS GUYS IN ENGLAND
AND ASKED THEM WHERE THEY WERE FAE
WAN SAID THAT HE WUS FAE CAMPSIE
AND THE ITHER TWO SAID THEY WERE SKINT TAE.

EFFELWYE CUTIE PIE

"THERE'S SKULLDUGGERRY AFOOT" SAID
SERGEANT ROSEBUD TO CONSTABLE SHOOEY GREEN
"THIS TOON IS FULL O' SCOUNDRELS
IT'S THE BUSIEST IT'S EVER BEEN"

"GET A HOD O' CONSTABLE BOOGIE BARCLAY
TELL HIM TAE KEEP AN EYE OAN THE DARROCH GANG
THEY'RE SURE TAE BE IN THAT COMMANCERO
WI' THEIR WINE WUMMIN AND SANG"

TWO DAYS EARLIER ONE HUNDRED STEAK PIES
WENT MISSING FROM THE COOPERATIVE STORE
AND ANGUS DARROCH WAS IN THE FRAME
SERGEANT ROSEBUD JUST COULD'NY TAKE IT ANYMORE

"I'LL HANG THAT DARROCH AND HIS GANG
FAE THE HIGHEST BLINKIN' TREE
AH'VE NEVER CAUGHT THE BLAGGARDS YIT
THEY'RE JOOST TOO FLY FOR ME"

CONSTABLE SHOOEY GREEN CAST HIS MIND BACK
TO THE DINNER HE ATE LAST NIGHT
IF SERGEANT ROSEBUD KNEW IT WAS STEAK PIE
HE WOULD BE SWINGING FAE THE POLIS LIGHT

BUT ALL THE STEAK PIES HAD BEEN DEVOURED
BY THE CAMPSIE FOLK IN THE KNOW
BUT THERE WAS ONE LEFT TO BE DELIVERED
TO A CERTAIN SERGEANT THAT WE ALL KNOW

AS SERGEANT ROSEBUD OPENED THE PACKAGE
HE TOOK A WHIFF OF THE LOVELY PIE
HE COULD NEVER RESIST THE TEMPTATION
AND FOR STEAK PIE HE WOULD SURELY DIE

A NOTE CAME WITH THE STEAK PIE, WHICH READ,
"DEAR SERGEANT ROSEBUD, MY LOVELY ADVERSARY
ENJOY YOUR STEAK, AND PLEASE DON'T CRY
FROM YOURS FAITHFULLY, EFFELWYE CUTIE PIE".

WHO'S ZOOMIN WHO

WHIT IT A' BOYLES DOON TAE SHUG
IS THAT OOR AIRLINE IS UP IN THE AIR
'N' WE'VE TOOK A' THE MUG'S MONEY
FOR WE DON'T GIE A SHIT OR CARE

"WE'RE NO' HONEST BUSINESS MEN SHUG
WE JUST TAKE TAKE TAKE
AND WE DON'T GIVE A MONKEY'S
FOR WE WANT ALL THE CAKE"

"SHOULD WE NO' FEEL SORRY JOHN
FOR TAKIN' POOR FOLK'S MONEY"
"OCH DON'T YOU BE DAFT SHUG
UR YE TRYING TAE BE FUNNY"

"DAE YE THINK IT WILL BE SAFE JOHN
FOR US TAE WALK DOON THE STREET
THERE'S A LOT OF ANGRY FOLK OUT THERE
YE NEVER KNOW WHO YOU'LL MEET

A HEARD TAM CRAVEN THE SCOTS POET
HAS LOST THREE HUNDFRED AND SIXTY QUID
'N' HE'S WELL GOT BY THE CAMPSIE TEEGAY
AND THAT LOT ARE NO' BLOODY STUPID

A HEARD THEY STIE OOT IN THE CAMPSIE HILLS
AND THEY DRINK BUCKIE 'N' STIE IN A BIG CAVE
AND THEY ARE RELATED TAE BIN LADEN 'N' CANNIBALS
AND SWAGGER ABOOT SINGIN' SCOTLAND THE BRAVE

"WELL IF THAT'S THE CASE AM OFF SHUG
THE CAMPSIE TEEGAY ULL NO' CATCH ME
AM SHOOTIN' THE CRAW TAE BARBADOS
FOR AM NO' SHORT OF A BAWBEE

Well all I can say to the Boyle brothers is, have a nice life and enjoy your ill gotten gains,
for I can assure you, you will pay for your GREED ONE WAY OR ANOTHER,
CAMPSIE TEEGAY YA BASS

HOKKAIDO

HE WHISKED HIS BRIDE AWAY
TO THE LAND OF THE RISING SUN
HE HAD FOUND TRUE LOVE AT LAST
HE KNEW SHE WAS THE ONE

THEIR MARRIAGE WUSNY BLISSED
BY CERTAIN PEOPLE THEY KNEW
BUT THEY KNEW IN THEIR HEARTS
IT WAS THE RIGHT THING TO DO

ACROSS THE OCEANS THEY TRAVELLED
THE NEW WHISKY TO DISTIL
AND IN A FEW YEARS THEY WOULD BE DRINKING
THE NEW SYNO SCOTTISH GILL

AND EVERY NIGHT HE WOULD ASK HER
AFTER A WEE DRAMMY OR TWO
"DO YOU STILL LOVE ME MY RITA"
"HOKKAIDO, OCH I DO, HOKKAIDO"

SO HERE'S TAE MASATAKA AND RITA
MAY THEIR PRECIOUS LOVE NEVER END
A MIXTURE OF ALL DIFFERENT CULTURES
IS SURELY A NOBLE BLEND

WAN LAST PUFF

"WHERE HAVE ALL THE ASHTRAYS GONE"
SAID THE SMOKER TO THE BARMAN
"THEY HAVE ALL LEFT WI' THE SMOKERS
IN THE BIG BLACK SEDAN"

"YE MEAN TAE SAY THERE'S NAE SMOKIN'
IN A' THE PUBS 'N' CLUBS 'N' BARS"
"THAT'S RIGHT M' FRIEND, NO' EVEN OAN BUSES
OR PRIVATE MOTOR CARS"

"WHIT'S THIS WORLD COMIN' TAE
WHEN IN THE PUB YE CANNY SMOKE"
"WELL, YIV GOT TAE LOOK EFTER YIR HEALTH SIR
THAT SMOKIN' WID MAKE YE BOAK"

"ACH WELL, GIES A PINT O' HEAVY
BUT AM DESPERATE FUR A FAG"
"OCH IT'S A' IN THE MIND SIR, HERE
PUT YIR CIGGIES IN THIS BIN BAG"

"WUD YE LET ME HUV WAN LAST PUFF
FUR THE SAKE OF AULD LANG SYNE"
"WELL ALRIGHT SIR, BUT JUST REMEMBER
IT'S YOUR LIFE AS WELL AS MINE"

THE VALLEY OF SIN

THERE WAS A WEE MAN
FAE PERU
WHO WAS A SALESMAN
FOR IRN-BRU

"IT'S THE HONEST MANS' DRINK"
HE WOULD OFTEN SAY
"KEEPS A MAN SOBER
HEALTHY AND TRUE"

HE WANDERED THE ANDES
WI' BIG BARNEY HIS DUG
AND EVERY NIGHT
THEY WOULD SLEEP OAN HIS RUG

AND THEN WAN NIGHT
HE REACHED THE VALLEY OF SIN
WHERE HE MET UP WI' A DASTARDLY RAPSCALLION
KNOWN LOCALLY AS THE "BIG YIN"

WHEN HE WOKE IN THE MORNING
OAN BIG BELLA'S RUG
HE KNEW RIGHT AWAY
HE'D BEEN TAKEN FUR A MUG

GUID SENSE HUD WENT OOT
AND GUID DRINK HUD WENT IN
AND THAT'S HOW IT GOES
IN THE VALLEY OF SIN

THE BAKER'S DAUGHTER

I MET HER AT GREGG'S THE BAKERS
NEXT TO THE STRAWBERRY TART STAND
AND TWENTY FOUR HOURS LATER
WE WERE WALKING HAND IN HAND

WE WENT FOR WALKS ALL OVER THE CAMPSIES
AND UP AND DOON SAUCHIEHALL STREET
AND SHE KEPT TELLIN' ME ABOOT HER BAKIN'
AS SHE SWEPT ME AFF M' FEET

M' TASTE BUDS WERE DAIN SOMMERSAULTS
WI' THOUGHTS O' HER LEMON MERINGUE PIES
AND A WUS A' OVERCOME WI' EMULSION
WHEN A LOOKED IN TAE HER MINCE PIES

THEN SHE LURED ME TAE HER HOUSE
WITH THE PROMISE OF TEA AND SCONES
AND VERY SOON THE BEDSPRINGS WOULD BE RATTLING
WI' THE SOUND O' FLESH AND BONES

SHE TEASED ME WI' HER APPLE TARTS
AND TRAINED ME TO BEG AND SIT
THEN SHE LED ME TAE THE PANTRY
AND MY GOD! A WUS LOVIN' IT

HER TOTTIE SCONES ARE MAGIC
AND HER RHUBARB CRUMBLE A DELIGHT
THANK GOD FOR GREGG'S THE BAKERS
FOR NOW WE'RE THE GITHER EVERY SINGLE NIGHT

KIDDIN' M' SELF OAN

A PHONED HER IN THE MORNIN'
THEN A PHONED HER UP AT NIGHT
A CANNY SEEM TO BE DOIN'
ANY BLOODY THING RIGHT

A PHONED HER FAE THE BUS STOP
THEN A PHONED HER FAE THE TRAIN
WHIT THE HELL IS SHE PLAYIN' AT
SHE'S DRIVIN' ME INSANE

THEN A PHONED HER FAE THE BOOZER
THEN A PHONED HER FAE THE LOO
THEN A PHONED HER FAE THE BLACK MARIA
WHAT ELSE WUS A TAE DO

THEN A PHONED M' BRITHER FUR BAIL MONEY
IT WID BE A SHORT TERM LOAN
THEN A THREW M'SEL IN THE CLYDE
A WUS KIDDIN' M' CELL PHONE

THE MIRROR MAN

OH MY GOD!
I'M RUNNIN' OOT O' TEETH
AH'LL HUV TAE PHONE UP THE BUTCHER
'N' CANCEL A' M' BEEF

OH MY GOD!
M' EYESIGHT'S GETTIN' WORSE
AH'LL HUV TAE PHONE UP THE OPTICIAN
OR PREFERABLY A NURSE

OH MY GOD!
M' HAIR IS FALLIN' OOT
AH'LL HUV TAE PHONE UP THE BIG MAN
BEFORE A LOOK LIKE A COOT

OH MY GOD!
AM RUNNIN' OOT O' BEER
AH'LL HUV TAE PHONE UP THE BREWERY
BUT IT'S TOO BLOODY DEAR

OH MY GOD!
AM HALF BLEEDIN' PISSED
A WUD PHONE UP GOD
BUT AM AN ATHEIST

NO MORE GAELIC COFFEES

A VOLATILE MIX OF CIRCUMSTANCES
LED ME TO A GREAT BIG SORE HEID
IT LASTED FOR THIRTY SIX HOURS
AND AT TIMES A THOUGHT A WUS DEID

THE CELTIC WUR PLAYIN' THE RANGERS
WHILST I WAS IN TENERIFE
AND IT WUS M' FIFTY NINTH BIRTHDAY
AS I TURNED OVER "ANITHER NEW LEAF"

IT STARTED AFF WI' JIST A FEW BEERS
THEN BACK TAE THE HOTEL FOR DINNER
BUT AFTER THE FIFTH BEER WENT DOON
I BECAME JUST ANOTHER SINNER

LATER ON AFTER A CELTIC VICTORY
THE GAELIC COFFEES STARTED TAE FLOW
AND A ENDED UP WI' A SENORITA
IN A PLACE A DID'NY KNOW

SHE POURED ME RED WINE WI' PROMISES
AND TOLD ME I WAS A SEXY GUY
WELL! SHE MUST HUV BEEN DRUNK TAE
SO I SAID "ADIOS SENORITA, ADIOS, BYE BYE"

AND NOW FORTY EIGHT HOURS LATER
I'M BEGINNING TO FEEL RATHER GOOD
SO THERE WILL BE NO MORE GAELIC COFFEES
I'LL JUST STICK TAE THE BEER AND THE FOOD

THE JAIKET

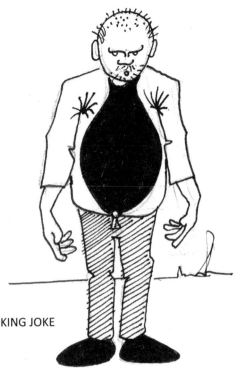

TRYING TO LOSE WEIGHT ISNY EASY
IN FACT SOMETIMES IT WOULD MAKE YE CRY
BUT EVERYTHING FELL INTO PLACE ONE DAY
WHEN A CERTAIN JAIKET I DID BUY

A TRIED IT OAN 'N' TRIED TAE ZIP IT UP
BUT M' BEER BELLY WOULD NOT ALLOW
AND SO A DECIDED RIGHT THERE AND THEN
IT'S HIGH TIME A MADE A WEE VOW

SO O'ER TAE KIRKIE BATHS A DID GO
WI' DETERMINATION OAN M' MIND
THE BEER BELLY WOULD HUV TAE GO
AND THE EXCESS POUNDS LEFT BEHIND

UP AND DOON THE LANES A SWAM
SHOWIN' AFF TAE A' THE FOLK
A WUS DETERMINED TAE BE SKINNY
BUT TRYING TAE LOSE WEIGHT WUS NAE BLINKING JOKE

NAE MERR CHOCOLATE OR FATTY FOODS
'N' NAE MERR ICE CREAM OR BEER
AND THEN A BEGAN TAE WONDER
JUST WHY THE HELL WE ARE ALL HERE

TEMPTATION WAS SOMETHING A COULD NEVER RESIST
AS A STRUGGLED TO LOSE THE WEIGHT
THEN A REMEMBERED MODERATION
AND THAT JAIKET WOULD HUV TAE WAIT

ACH TAKE YIR TIME TAM
A KEPT SAYIN' TAE M'SEL
DON'T GIE UP THE THINGS YE LOVE
FOR PEACE OF MIND CAN KEEP YOU WELL

WE ARE ALL A WEE BIT CONSCIOUS ON THE OUTSIDE
AND HOW WE SHOULD APPEAR
BUT WE REALLY SHOULD BE LOOKING INWARDS
THAT'S WHY GOD PUT US ALL HERE

SO I HAVE COME TO THE CONCLUSION
THAT THERE WILL BE NO MORE WEIGHT LOSS CRIES
AND I'VE GIVEN THE JAIKET BACK TAE JAMES CURTIS
AND TOLD HIM TO GET ME A BIGGER SIZE

LET'S BE PRETENTIOUS THE GITHER

TAKE YIR HAUN AFF THERE BIG MAN
YE KNOW AM SENSITIVE TAE YIR TOUCH"
"OCH C'MON JEMIMA MY DARLING
YE KNOW A LOVE YOU SO VERY MUCH"

"QUOTE ME WAN O' YIR POEMS BIG MAN
'N' AH'LL CONSIDER YIR RANDINESS
YE KNOW A LOVE THE WAY YE TALK
YOU'VE GOT AN OFFAY LOT O' FINESSE"

"'N' POUR ME ANITHER GLESS O' CHAMPAGNY
IT'S MAKIN' ME FEEL AWFY GUID
'N' GIE ME SOME MERR O' THEY FISHES EGGS
A KNOW YIR WORTH A RIGHT FEW QUID"

"SO LET'S BE PRETENTIOUS THE GITHER BIG MAN
AND WE'LL LEAVE THE WORLD FAR BEHIND
AND DON'T THINK MA HEID IS BUTTONED UP THE BACK
FOR A KNOW EXACTLY WHAT'S ON YOUR MIND"

BETWEEN AND BETWIXED

FLY ME TO DUNOON
AND LET ME DRINK IN ALL THE BARS
KEEP THE BEVVY FLOWIN'
AFORE WE SHOOT AFF TAE MARS

FILL M' GLESS WI' WHISKY
'N' M' ITHER WAN WI' BEER
DRINK IS ALL A LIVE FUR
BUT IT'S TOO BLOODY DEAR

IN OTHER WORDS
I'M A COSMONAUT
IN OTHER WORDS
A CANNY GET CAUGHT

FLY ME ROON THE COSMOS
AND LET ME LOOK FOR OTHER LIFE
AH'LL DAE ANYTHING TAE GET AWAY
FROM THE WIFE

IN OTHER WORDS
I'M BETWEEN AND BETWIXED
IN OTHER WORDS
HOW'RE YE FIXED

BIG ANN AND THE WEE MAN

BIG ANN WENT IN TAE THE VAN
LOOKING FOR THE WEE MAN
THE WEE MAN WAS DOON IN THE PUB
DRINKING A BLACK AND TAN

'WHIT'S HIS GAME?' THOUGHT BIG ANN
AS SHE LAY ON THE BIG BLACK DIVAN
'AH'LL SORT HIM OOT
THAT DASTARDLY WEE MAN"

THE WEE MAN FINISHED HIS TENTH BLACK 'N' TAN
AND SHOUTED, "CHEERIO BOYS!
I'M OFF TAE SEE BIG ANN
UP IN THE BIG BLACK DIVAN IN THE VAN"

AS THE WEE MAN SNEAKED IN TAE THE VAN
HE GOT WALLOPED OAN THE HEID WI' A CAN
AND THAT WUS THE END
O' THE WEE MAN AND BIG ANN

YIR MONEY OR YIR LIFE,
OR YIR BLACK PUDDIN' SUPPER

WHENEVER NOTHING SEEMS TO BE GOING RIGHT
A ALWAYS SEEM TAE TAKE TAE THE DRINK
BUT THAT NIGHT A DIDNY GO TAE THE PUB
A NEEDED SOME TIME TAE THINK

THE AROMA OF THE LOCAL CHIP SHOP
REMINDED MY STOMACH I NEEDED FOOD
AND SO A BLACK PUDDIN' SUPPER WAS PURCHASED
AND BY JINGS IT SMELLED GOOD

A HUD LEARNED A GOOD LESSON
A LONG TIME AGO
THAT WHILST WALKING THE STREETS OF GLASGOW
HOW TAE HOD OAN TAE M' DOUGH

HE CAME AT ME OUT OF THE BLUE
AND POINTED THE GUN AT MY HEART
"YOUR MONEY OR YOUR LIFE", HE SHOUTED
"PISS OFF", I SAID, "YOU LITTLE FART"

"DON'T THINK AM KIDDIN' MISTER
FOR THIS IS A REAL GUN,
SO GET YIR EFFIN MONEY OOT
AM NO' DAIN THIS FIR FUN"

"A JOOST BOUGHT A BLACK PUDDIN' SUPPER". SAYS I
"WI' M' LAST THREE AND A HALF QUID
'N' IF YOU THINK AH'VE GOT ANY MONEY PAL
WELL, YE MUST BE BLOODY STUPID"

"LOOK! JOOST STAND AND DELIVER MISTER
YIR MONEY OR YIR LIFE
'N' GIES WAN O' THE CHIPS
UR'LL STAB YE WI' M' KNIFE"

"THAT'S NO' A REAL KNIFE, IS IT?
"NO IT'S ONLY A KID OAN WAN
GIES A BIT O' THAT BLACK PUDDIN' SUPPER
AM ABSOLUTELY STARVIN"

"HOW COME YIV NAE MONEY
YE LOOK LIKE YIR WORTH A FEW BOB"
"OCH M' WIFE HUS JUST LEFT ME
AND A GOT PAYED AFF FAE M' JOB

'N' NOO THE MORTGAGE CANNY BE PAYED
AND AM OOT OAN THE STREET
'N' IT'S GONNY BE A LONG TIME
TAE A CAN AFFORD A BIT O' MEAT"

"TRUST ME TAE PICK SOMEBODY THAT'S SKINT
FIR AM NO' THAT GOOD AT MUGGIN' FOLK
TAE TELL YE THE TRUTH MISTER
A ONLY DAE IT FIR A JOKE"

"A JOKE IS IT! A JOKE! UR YE NUTS
YIV ATE HAUF M' BLACK PUDDIN' SUPPER
'N' NOO AH'VE NO' GOT A PENNY
'N' AM OAN THE STREET LIKE A PAUPER

"OCH DINNY YOU BE SAD MISTER
FOR AM NO' REALLY A BAD GUY
HERE'S A TENNER FOR YOUR TROUBLE
AH'LL JOOST SHOOT THE CRAW AND SAY GOODBYE"

AS THE LITTLE FART SPROCKLED AWAY
I THANKED HIM FOR THE TENNER SUB
THEN SLIPPED IT IN TAE M' WALLET WI' IT'S COUSINS
AND THOUGHT WHIT THE HELL, AND SAUNTERED DOON TAE THE PUB.

THE STARVIN' SERGEANT

ALL THE GOSSIP MONGERS WERE BLUSTERING
AS THE RUMOURS SPREAD A' OE'R THE TOON
IT SEEMS THAT YOUNG TAMMY TROOT
HAS FLED AULD CAMPSIE TOON

FOUR DIZZEN SQUARE SAUSAGES WENT MISSIN'
FAE MACDONALD'S BUTCHER'S UP THE STREET
AND NOW THE LOCAL KEYSTONE COPS
WERE STARTING TAE FLEX THEIR FEET

"WE WILL TRACK THIS SAUSAGE THIEF DOON"
SAID SERGEANT ROSEBUD WI' A HUNGRY GRIN
"AH'VE BEEN DEPRIVED O' M' SUPPER
THAT TAMMY TROOT HAS COMMITTED A TERRIBLE SIN

"WE WILL SEARCH EVERY NOOK AND CRANNY
AND SMOKE THIS TAMMY TROOT OOT
YE CAN RELY OAN THE LOCAL POLIS,
FOR WE KNOW ALL THE DODGERS INSIDE OOT"

THE POLIS SURROUNDED THE BURNS TAVERN
WHERE THE INFAMOUS DARROCH GANG HUNG OOT
"OK DARROCH" SAID SERGEANT ROSEBUD,
"YOU KNOW WHAT THIS IS ALL ABOOT"

"A DON'T KNOW WHIT YIR OAN ABOOT SARGE"
SAID ANGUS DARROCH WI' A SAUSAGE SMILE
"YOUNG TAMMY TROOT IS INNOCENT,
FOR TO STEAL IS NO' THE BOY'S STYLE"

A SMELL O' SAUSAGE AND INGINS
WAS WAFTING THROUGHOUT THE PUB
AND SERGEANT ROSEBUDS TASTEBUDS WERE BOUNCING
HE JUST HAD TO HAVE SOME GRUB

SUDDENLY TWO ROLLS AND SAUSAGE APPEARED
AND SERGEANT ROSEBUD COULD NO LONGER WAIT
"GOD BLESS TAMMY TROOT", HE SHOUTED
AS HE DEVOURED THE ROLLS AND THE PAPER PLATE

BARNEY COOL

A WUS STANDIN' WAITIN' IN THE QUEUE
OOTSIDE HEAVENS LOVELY GATE
NEXT TO A WEE JACK RUSSELL NAMED SHUG
WHO WAS IN AN AWFY DISHEVELLED STATE

"WHIT'S THE MATTER WI' YOU WEE MAN"
A WHISPERED IN HIS LUG
"AM WEE SHUG FAE THE SOU' SIDE BIG MAN
THEY'LL NO' TAKE ME FOR A MUG"

HE BLETHERED OAN ABOOT HIS LIFE
AND ALL HIS TROUBLES AND WOES
AND SAYS HE'D BITTEN TEN POSTMEN
AND A POLISMAN OAN THE NOSE

THEN THE ANGELS CAME TO GET THE WEE MAN
FOR THERE WAS NO PLACE TO HIDE
"TAKE YIR HAUNS AFF ME" HE SHOUTED
"AM WEE SHUG FAE THE SOU' SIDE"

THERE WAS AN AWFY SHOUTING AND A HOWLING
AS BARNEY LISTENED TO WEE SHUGS YELL
THEN HE HEARD A BIG DOOR BANG
AS THEY TOOK HIM DOON TAE HELL

A COULD'NT UNDERSTAND
WHY HE WAS SO ANGRY
FOR I'D HAD A GOOD LIFE
WITH A LOVELY FAMILY

I'D GO FOR GREAT WALKS WI' MA MASTER
AND BIG TAM FAE CAMPSIE
AND LISTEN TAE THEIR DAFT PATTER
SITTIN' AT THE SEVENTEENTH TEE

A DOGS LIFE IS A SWIFT ONE
SEVEN TIMES QUICKER THAN HIS MASTER
BUT SOME DOGS ARE LIKE HUMANS
THEY WANT EVERYTHING DONE FASTER

THE LEEK

MY OLD FRIEND BILL
HE GAVE ME A LEEK
AND A MADE A POT O' SOUP
THAT NORMALLY LASTED A WEEK

WHEN THE SOUP WAS READY
THERE WAS A KNOCK OAN MA DOOR
IT WUS BILL WI' A' HIS WEANS
AND THERE WUS MERR THAN THREE OR FOUR

THEY A' GOT STUCK IN
TAE THE LOVELY MINESTRONE
A WANTID TAE KEEP SOME FUR THE MORRA
NOO THERE WUSNY GONNY BE OANY

NOT A SLICE O' BREED
WUS LEFT IN MA HOOSE
NO' EVEN A FEW CRUMBS
TAE FEED A WEE MOOSE

BUT GUID AULD SCOTS HOSPITALITY
IS UNBROKEN AND RENOWNED
IT'S ALL OVER THE WORLD
MORE SOLID THAN A POUND

MY OLD FRIEND BILL
HE GAVE ME ANITHER LEEK
AND SAYS; "YIR SOUP WUS MAGIC TAM,
SAME TIME NIXT WEEK."

I wrote this poem for Bill Torrance at Saga Radio.

Well, he thought, you can fool some of the people all of the time, and all of the people some of the time, which is just long enough to be the President of the United States.
Spike Milligan, 1963.

There is hardly a single person in the House of Commons worth painting; although some of them would be better with a little white-washing.
Oscar Wilde, 1891.

THE TARTAN AMANS

A WOMAN CALLED AMAN
MARRIED A MAN CALLED AMAN
AND THEY HUD A WEE BOY
AND THEY CAW'D HIM BIG STAN

THEN ALANG CAME A SISTER
WHO THEY CAW'D JEAN AMAN
AND ANITHER TEN BRITHERS
BUT THAT WUSNY REALLY THE PLAN

THEY ALL TOOK TAE FITBA
AND WHAT A RARE SIGHT TO SEE
ELEVEN SCOTTISH ASIANS
PLAYING FOR THEIR COUNTRY

AND TO THE WORLD CUP FINAL
THE SCOTS ASIANS DID REACH
AND TROUNCED THE BRAZILIANS
WHO HAD LEARN'T FITBA OAN THE BEACH

THEN ALL THE AMANS DRANK FROM THE WORLD CUP
TRUE SCOTSMEN IN EVERY WAY
AMANS A MAN FOR A' THAT
IS THERE ANY MORE TO SAY

Way back in 1982 I was on holiday in Toronto and I was staying with my uncle John Craven and his wife Anne. One morning I went for a walk and I came across a game of soccer inside a school. You must remember that Toronto has every nationality in the world living there. It was an under 16s football match and there were some really great players. I walked over to the touchline and I heard the coach shouting at a wee Japanese boy on the right wing.
"Go for it Sean, go for it".
I thought Sean, must be a Japanese name.
"Excuse me". I said to the coach. "That wee Japanese boy is some player, what's his name?"
"That's Sean Fitzpatrick"
"Yir kiddin'"
"No, his father is Irish and his mother is Japanese"
"Is that no' fantastic, brilliant".
"Sure is".

SOME MORE LIES

A FISHERMAN WENT TO PLAY AT GOLF
AND A GOLFER WENT TO FISH
THEN THEY BOTH ENDED UP IN THE NINETEENTH HOLE
WHERE THEY TALKED A LOAD OF PISH

THE FISHERMAN SAID HE HAD GOT AN EAGLE
AND THE GOLFER SAID WELL DONE
THEN THE GOLFER SAID HE HAD CAUGHT A TEN POUNDER
AND SO THE LIES WERE BEING SPUN

THE GOLFER SAID HE WAS FILTHY RICH
THE FISHERMAN SAID HE WAS POOR
THEN THEY SLAPPED EACH OTHER OAN THE BACK
AND GOT RID OF THE DAILY STOOR

AND SO THE DRINK FLOWED DOWN
LONG IN TO THE NIGHT
AND THE NEW FOUND FRIENDS
GREW HELLUVA TIGHT

THERE WAS A TWENTY TWO FOOT SALMON
AND ALBATROSSES GALORE
AND HANDSHAKES WITH PROMISES
AND THE WILD ROVER NO NEVER NO MORE

THEY SAID THEIR FAREWELLS
UNDERNEATH THE DARKEN SKIES
AND MADE PLANS TO MEET AGAIN
TO TELL SOME MORE LIES

Written on New Years Eve at the seventeenth tee at the Campsie Golf Course after talking to an old friend Victor McClaren, "one of the greatest golfers in the world".

Believe me, at my age it's hard to find anything I haven't done before and even harder to do it.
George Burns.

I recently turned sixty. Practically a third of my life is over.
Woody Allen.
She said she was approaching forty, and I couldn't help wondering from what end.
Bob Hope.

Tonight we honour a man old enough to be his own father.
George Burns.